Shapes Around Us

Daniel Nunn

Raintree

Chicago, Illinois

www.capstonepub.com
Visit our website to find out more information about Heinemann-Raintree books.

To order:

☎ Phone 800-747-4992

▣ Visit www.capstonepub.com to browse our catalog and order online.

© 2012 Raintree
an imprint of Capstone Global Library, LLC
Chicago, Illinois

Edited by Daniel Nunn, Rebecca Rissman, and Sian Smith
Designed by Joanna Hinton-Malivoire
Picture research by Elizabeth Alexander
Illustrations by Joanna Hinton-Malivoire
Originated by Capstone Global Library Ltd.
Production by Victoria Fitzgerald
Printed and bound in China by South China Printing Company Ltd

15 14 13 12 11
10 9 8 7 6 5 4 3 2 1

Library of Congress Cataloging-in-Publication Data
Nunn, Daniel.
 Shapes around us / Daniel Nunn.
   p. cm.—(Math every day)
 Includes bibliographical references and index.
 ISBN 978-1-4329-5732-2 (hb)—ISBN 978-1-4329-5737-7 (pb)
 1. Shapes—Juvenile literature. I. Title.
 QA445.5.N86 2012
 516'.15—dc23   2011013020

Acknowledgments
We would like to thank the following for permission to reproduce photographs: Dreamstime.com p.13 (© Raphotography); Shutterstock pp.4 left (© Africa Studio), 4 right (© Lori Sparkia), 5 left (© erperlstrom), 5 right (© Coprid), 7 (© Dmitriy Shironosov), 8 (© Chiyacat), 8 (© Tilo G), 8 (© Carlos Caetano), 8 (© akiyoko), 8 (© Jiang Hongyan), 8 (© Kristina Postnikova), 9 (© Beneda Miroslav), 11 (© Anna Chelnokova), 12 (© Jiri Hera), 12 (© Konstantin Yolshin), 12 (© Evgeny Karandaev), 12 (© Dmitry Naumov), 12 (© Swapan), 16, 17 (© Mariia Sats), 20, 21 (© karamysh).

Cover photograph of a Palheiro Traditional thatched house, Santana village, Madeira reproduced with permission of Alamy (© STOCKFOLIO®).

Contents

Shapes Around Us

Let's look for shapes.
It's time to play!

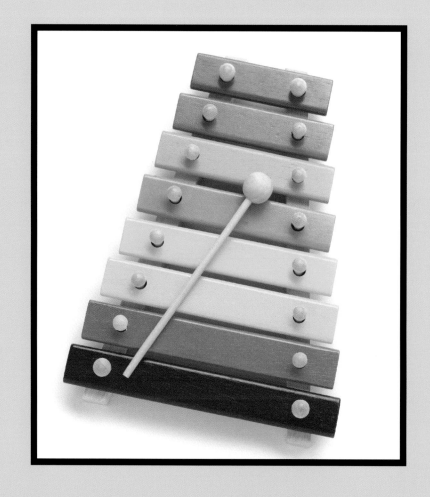

How many shapes can
you find today?

Circles

This is a circle.
Circles are round.

Look at this photo.
How many have you found?

Circles, circles, everywhere!

Is this window a circle?

No, it's a square!

Squares

1

4

2

Squares have
four sides, all
the same size!

3

How many squares are here?

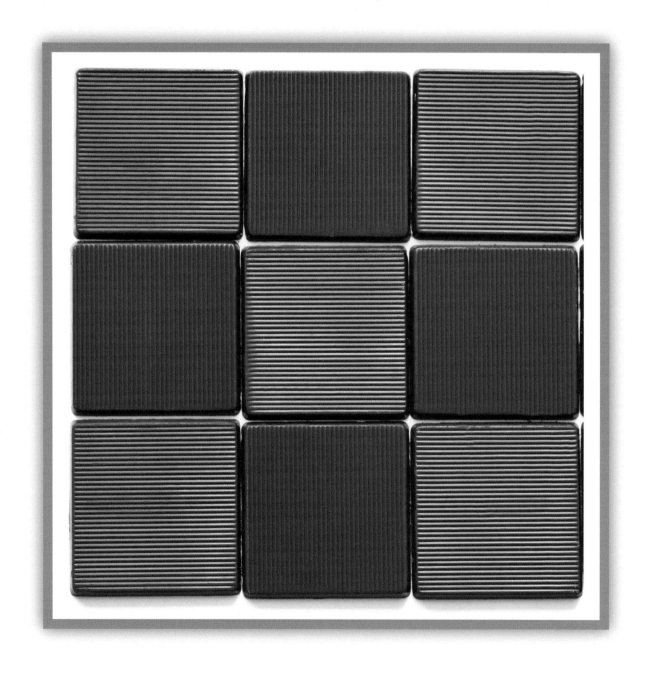

Look with your eyes!

Here are some more squares,
both big squares and small.

Are there squares on this cake?
Try and count them all.

Rectangles

long side

short side

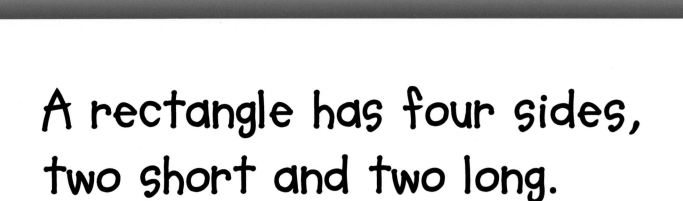

A rectangle has four sides,
two short and two long.

NOT A RECTANGLE

If you think it's got six sides,
I'm afraid you'd be wrong!

15

Can you see any rectangles by this front door?

I can see at least three, can you see any more?

Triangles

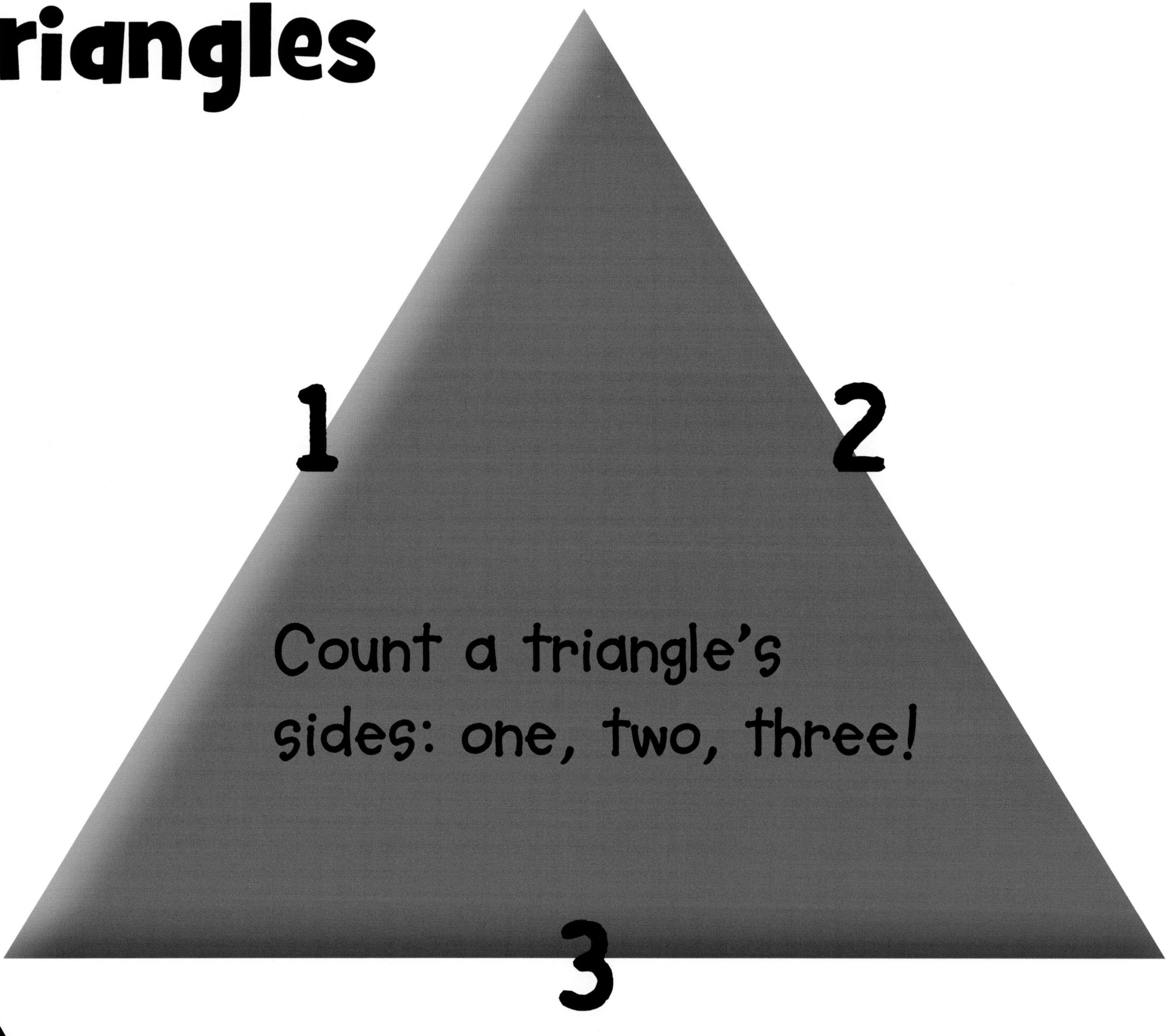

1

2

Count a triangle's
sides: one, two, three!

3

How many points does it have?
Can you see?

point

19

Look at this picture.
Are there triangles here?

20

If you found at least three,
then I'll give you a cheer!

Other Shapes

Are there other shapes, too?
Yes, of course there are!

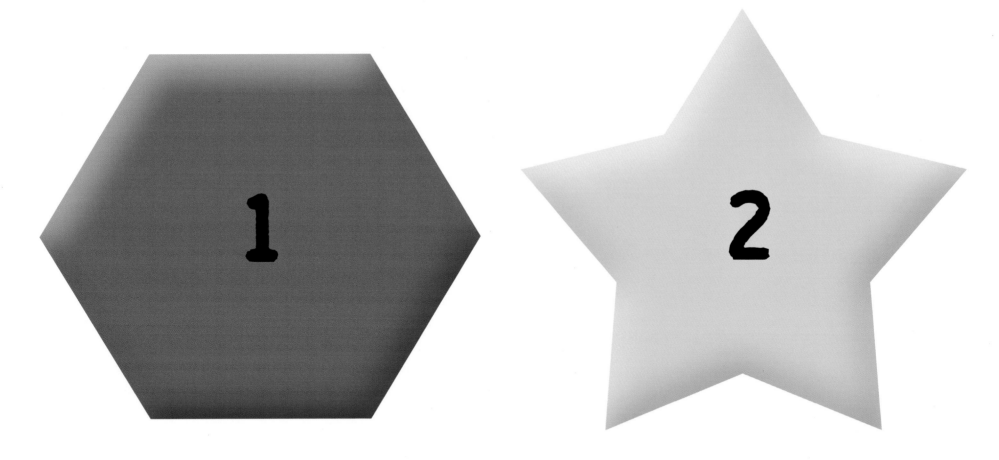

Do you know the names
of these shapes?

If you do, you're a star...

(And a star is a shape too!)

Answers on page 24

Index

Answer to question on page 22

Shape 1 is a hexagon.

Shape 2 is a star.

Shape 3 is a diamond.

Shape 4 is an oval.